THE HOLOCAUST

The Holocaust 1939-1946

Stuart A. Kallen

Published by Abdo & Daughters, 4940 Viking Drive, Suite 622, Edina, Minnesota 55435.

Library bound edition distributed by Rockbottom Books, Pentagon Tower, P.O. Box 36036, Minneapolis, Minnesota 55435.

Printed in the United States.

Cover Photo credit: Bettmann Archives
Interior Photo credits: Bettmann Archives, pages 7, 8, 9, 20, 21, 22, 29, 31, 37, 44, 50, 55, 59
Archive Photos, pages 15, 18, 32, 37, 52
Wide World, pages 7, 13, 16, 40, 43

Edited By Rosemary Wallner

Library of Congress Cataloging-in-Publication Data

Kallen, Stuart A., 1955-
    The Holocaust, 1939-1946 / Stuart A. Kallen.
        p.   cm. -- (The Holocaust)
    Includes Bibliographical references and index.
    ISBN 1-56239-352-9
    1. Holocaust, Jewish (1939-1946) -- Juvenile literature.
    [1. Holocaust, Jewish (1939-1946)] I. Title. II. Series:
    Holocaust (Edina, Minn.)
    D804.3.K35   1994
    940.53'18--dc20   94-19480
                                                                CIP
                                                                AC

Table of Contents

FOREWORD

The Holocaust is a tragic time in world history. It was a time of prejudice and bias turned to hate and the persecution of an ethnic group by persons who came into a position of power, allowing them to carry out that hate.

The Holocaust series depicts what prejudice and biases can lead to; how men, women and children—simply because they were Jewish—died horrible deaths.

When a child is born it has no prejudices. Bias must be learned and someone has to display it.

The goal of this series is to enlighten children and help them recognize the ignorance of prejudice so that future generations will be tolerant, understanding, compassionate, and free of prejudice.

Acknowledgments:

Rabbi Morris Allen
        Beth Jacob Congregation

Dr. Stewart Ross
        Mankato State University

Special Thanks to The United States Holocaust Memorial Museum

CHAPTER ONE

THE STORY OF A NIGHTMARE

*T*his is the story of a nightmare. A nightmare that really happened. A nightmare that lasted twelve years. A nightmare in which six million people were murdered in factory death camps simply because they were Jewish. They were murdered because Adolf Hitler and German Nazis hated all Jews. That was the only reason for their death.

This nightmare happened while the nations of the world were fighting in World War II. That war took millions of lives all over the world, not only Jews. Tens of millions of innocent victims died including Gypsies, homosexuals, Jehovah's Witnesses, Catholics, and the physically and mentally disabled. In fact anyone who opposed the Nazis was sent to a death camp. But as a survivor of the nightmare, writer Elie Wiesel said, "Not all victims were Jewish, but all Jews were victims."

Reading about this period in history is not easy. The details are horrible. But the story cannot be made pretty. And it must be told. For if people forget, such a nightmare can happen again. And it is our duty as human beings to see that it does not. So when you read about this nightmare, remember that it happened only fifty years ago. And then vow to yourself that such a nightmare will never happen again.

CHAPTER TWO

THE NAZI DREAM OF POWER

*I*n 1933 Adolf Hitler and the Nazi Party seized the reins of power in Germany. Hitler was wildly popular with the common people. He preached a program of full employment, German patriotism, and total obedience to himself, *der Fürher*. He also preached a message of hatred directed towards Jewish people.

Aided by his propaganda minister, Joseph Goebbels, Hitler took total control of the hearts and minds of the German people. Hitler was elevated to god-like status whose word was law. Hitler banished all political parties except the Nazi Party. He also stripped away the civil liberties of the German people. And with the stroke of his pen, he stripped away the right of every Jew in Germany to live in peace.

Jews became despised outsiders in their own country. Their temples and books were burned. Their businesses were seized by crazed mobs. Jewish men, women, and children were sent to concentration camps. They were forbidden to own radios, use telephones, have pets, or go to barbers or beauty salons. They could not buy food, go to school, or use swimming pools. Between 1933 and 1939 four hundred separate laws were passed to define, isolate, exclude, segregate, and impoverish German Jews.

And this hatred and discrimination was only a warm-up. These acts were a warm-up for one of the most horrible events in human history—as the Nazis put it: The Final Solution to the Problem of the Jews.

Hitler and his henchmen were ready to round up every man, woman, and child of Jewish heritage and send them to hideous deaths inside factory-style death camps. This is how it happened.

Der Fürher, Adolf Hitler, gives the Nazi salute from the Chancellory balcony in Berlin, Germany, 1939.

The 28th Nazi Brigade listening to Hitler's speech in Berlin, Germany, 1934.

CHAPTER THREE

AUSTRIA WELCOMES HITLER

*H*itler had other plans besides the destruction of the Jews. He wanted Germany to rule all of Europe—and then take over the world. On March 12, 1938, German soldiers marched into the neighboring country of Austria. Instead of receiving a fight, the Austrians welcomed the Nazis in the streets with flowers. To Hitler's surprise, most Austrians hated the Jews even more than he did. The Austrians wanted to become one with Hitler's dream of a world ruled by Aryan men. The 185,000 Jews living there—most of them in Vienna— were doomed.

Nazi storm troopers persecuting Jews in the streets of Berlin.

Nazi parade in pre-World War II Germany. All onlookers salute.

Hitler quickly set to work to terrorize Austria's Jews. He used his shock troops, the *Schutzstaffel* or SS for this purpose. The SS was the black-shirted security squad of elite Nazis—headed by Heinrich Himmler. The symbol of the SS was a skull and crossbones and they carried out Hitler's dirty work with frightening zeal.

The Austrian SS marked all shops owned by Jews. They ordered Austrians not to buy there. If someone was caught shopping at a Jewish store, they were made to parade through the streets wearing a sign that read: "I, Aryan Swine, Have Bought in a Jewish Shop."

As soon as Germany took over, Jews were attacked in the streets. The beards of pious Jews were forcibly shaved. Jewish women were forced to scrub gutters on their hands and knees while crowds mocked them. Jews were taken to the park and made to eat grass. They were forced to run in the streets until they fainted. Thousands of Jewish businesses were seized within a few weeks. Jews were thrown out of their homes and apartments. A concentration camp to imprison Jewish people was quickly set up in the Austrian town of Mauthausen.

By the summer of 1939, twenty-one thousand Jewish businesses had been transferred to non-Jewish ownership. By September, 75 percent of Vienna's Jews had left the country. Little did they know that within a few years, the Nazis would find the Jews wherever they were on the European continent. For the rest of Austria's Jews who couldn't leave, the nightmare had already begun.

CHAPTER FOUR

THE WORLD TURNS ITS BACK ON THE JEWS

*I*n the summer of 1938, a conference was held in the resort city of Evian, France. The conference was attended by delegates of thirty-two countries. The purpose of the conference was the "refugee crisis" in Europe. The true purpose was to decide what to do with the quarter-million Jews who Hitler wanted "banished" from Germany and Austria.

The conference was called by U. S. President Franklin Roosevelt. But before it was even held, every country involved was told that they would not have to change their immigration quotas. This meant that the Jewish "problem" would be discussed. But no country would have to open its doors to the hundreds of thousands of Jews made homeless by Hitler. Instead of sending a respected government official, Roosevelt sent one of his businessmen-friends to represent the United States.

Hitler issued a typical Nazi-style statement:

> I can only hope that the other world which has such deep sympathy for these criminals (the Jews) will at least be generous enough to convert this sympathy into practical aid. We on our part are ready to put all these criminals at the disposal of these countries, for all I care, even on luxury ships.

For nine days, the delegates met at a luxurious hotel on Lake Geneva in the French Alps. Each delegate rose in turn to express his sympathy for the plight of the Jews. Then each one offered a list of excuses for why his country could not possibly help. Most of the time, the delegates wiled away the hours water skiing, gambling, taking mineral baths, and riding horses.

Great Britain said it had no room on its tiny island for the Jews. To open Palestine (which they controlled) would upset the Arab nations. The British depended on the Arabs for oil.

The United States spoke about "political refugees," not Jewish people. They could not change their immigration quotas. Even Jewish children would not be allowed in—even if they were supported by private donations. In a poll of Americans taken at the time, 60 percent thought "Jews had bad qualities." Nearly half thought "Jews had too much power."

Twenty percent said that they sided with Hitler. In poll after poll, Americans said that they thought Jews were a threat to the United States.

The Australians said, "We don't have a racial problem and we don't want to import one."

Canada, mired in the Depression, said of the Jews, "none was too many." Canada would, however, accept farmers. This was of no help to the Jews, almost all of whom were city dwellers.

Columbia and Venezuela expressed sympathy, but no hope.

Holland and Denmark offered temporary asylum for a few refugees.

Only the Dominican Republic offered to take 100,000 Jews. But in the end, their relief agencies were so overwhelmed that few Jews were able to take advantage of the offer.

It was clear, nobody wanted the Jews. At the end of the conference, the German Foreign Office gloated in a letter that read:

> Since in many countries it was recently regarded as wholly incomprehensible why Germany did not wish to preserve a population element like the Jews...it appears astounding that countries seem in no way anxious to make use of these elements themselves now that opportunity offers.

In other words, the letter said, how can the world blame us for not wanting the Jews, when no one else in the world wants them either. If Germany wanted to be what it called *Judenrein* (cleansed of Jews) it would have to solve the problem by other means.

Hundreds of signs reading "Jews Not Wanted In This Place" were posted throughout Germany. This is the small town of Schwedt, Germany, 1938.

CHAPTER FIVE

THE FALL OF CZECHOSLOVAKIA

"War is life. War is the origin of all things." —Adolf Hitler.

*I*n March 1939, German soldiers invaded Czechoslovakia. Like the Austrian takeover, the Nazis didn't have to fire a shot. Czechoslovakia was one of the wealthiest and most democratic countries in central Europe. But British Prime Minister Neville Chamberlain had cut a deal with Hitler. Great Britain would not protect Czechoslovakia, with whom they had a treaty. Hitler, in turn, promised that the Nazis would not take over any other country. This was called a "policy of appeasement." Chamberlain thought he was saving his country from war with Germany. Soon, the world would regret Britain's appeasement with the vicious dictator.

Meanwhile, the German economy was growing, in part because of the assets seized from the Jews. As more and more German factories opened, there were not enough workers to keep them running. Adolf Eichmann, the head of the Gestapo's Jewish section, had a solution. Strong, young Czech Jews were sent to concentration camps in Germany to work as slaves.

Prime Minister of Great Britain, Neville Chamberlain, with Adolf Hitler, 1938.

CHAPTER SIX

WORLD WAR II BEGINS

*O*n September 1, 1939, the Nazi army struck again—this time it was Poland. Before the month was over, Poland had surrendered to the Nazis. In one short month more than twenty-two million people were added to the Nazi empire. Three-and-a-half million of them were Jews.

Poland had treaties with France and England. This time there would be no appeasement. France and Great Britain declared war on Germany. World War II had begun.

Poland was full of Jews who had lived there for centuries. And thousands of Jews had fled there from Germany, Austria, and Czechoslovakia, hoping to find safety from the Nazis. Once more they had to flee. Jews streamed out of cities and towns totting bundles and pushing carts with their belongings. They were headed anywhere that the Germans had yet to invade.

Jewish man in Berlin, Germany, 1940, is forced to wear the Star of David as a badge of identification.

In Poland the Nazis used the same tactics they had used in Germany to persecute the Jews. Jews were forced to sew a large, yellow, six-pointed Star of David on their clothes. They had to tip their hats to Germans in the street and get off the sidewalk when a German passed. The Germans cut the beards of pious Jews and made Jews do push-ups on the sidewalk. They made Jews spit on sacred objects in their temples. They made young Jewish women clean toilets with their hands.

On January 30, 1939, Hitler held a rally to celebrate his six years in power. He issued a warning, incredibly enough, blaming the Jews for the pending war. He said:

> If...Jewry inside and outside of Europe should succeed once more in plunging nations into another world war, the consequence will not be...the victory of Jewry, but the annihilation of the Jewish race in Europe.

On April 9, 1940, Germany invaded Denmark and Norway. Both countries quickly fell. On May 10, German armies swept across Belgium and the Netherlands. The Netherlands fell in five days. Belgium lasted three weeks. A quarter million British soldiers stationed there fled back to England across the English Channel from Dunkerque. On June 13, Paris, France, fell to the Nazis. Northern France was occupied by Germany. Southern France was occupied by Germany's ally, Italy.

During the summer of 1940, the German air force, or the *Luftwaffe,* launched massive bombing raids on Great Britain. Between July and October, the skies above England roared with the sound of Nazi bombers. The streets of England's great cities were ablaze from the bombs.

As Hitler had conquered Western Europe, he had plans for the East. In the spring of 1941, Greece, Yugoslavia, Bulgaria, and Romania fell to the Nazis. On the entire European continent, only the Soviet Union was left to repel the Nazis. Realizing the dream of dozens of dictators throughout history, Hitler had conquered most of Europe.

Hitler with Italian leader, Benito Mussolini.

CHAPTER SEVEN

THE VIOLATION OF POLAND

*H*itler justified the invasion of Poland with Germany's need for *lebensraum*, or "living space." The Poles were considered "subhuman" and Hitler wanted each and every one of them dead. German settlers were moved into Poland and the native Polish— and Jewish—populations were made slaves or forcibly removed. Cities and towns were renamed with German names. Mass slaughter of Catholic priests, intellectuals, and politicians was ordered.

The Nazis invaded Poland's ancient universities and killed all the professors. Historical archives were plundered. Art was stolen. National treasures were taken to Germany. Children who had blond hair and blue eyes—perfect Aryan features—were kidnapped and taken to Germany for "training." All other children were forbidden to go to school after fourth grade.

Men, women, and children who were physically or mentally disabled, or insane were rounded up and killed. Families of those killed were told that their relatives were getting the finest medical care. SS soldiers donned white doctor's coats to continue the charade. Real doctors and psychiatrists went along with the Nazis, using their professional knowledge to slaughter the innocents.

With all the killing going on, Hitler and the Nazis needed new methods for murdering people. Starvation was too slow. Drugs were too expensive. A method was devised where twenty people would be taken to a room and told that they were going to take showers. But the showerheads dispensed the poison gas hydrochloric acid, not water. Afterwards, the bodies would be burned, or cremated, in ovens, called crematoria. The lethal gas was made by Germany's most brilliant scientists in the country's largest chemical factories.

These methods of mass murder perfected on the disabled were later used to kill over six million Jews and four million other people.

A crematorium in a Nazi concentration camp at Weimar, Germany, containing the bones of women prisoners, discovered by American troops at the end of World War II.

The Nazi powers settled into their control over Western Europe. Anti-Jewish policy followed the same models perfected by Hitler in Germany and Austria. First, Jews were put into a separate category from everyone else. Then their civil liberties were restricted and their property was seized. Next, Jews were fired from jobs in government and as teachers in schools or universities. Jewish businesses were taken over. Then Jews were forced to live in separate neighborhoods, called ghettos, and wear large, yellow Star-of-David symbols.

By 1942 Jews were rounded up, taken to transit camps, packed into cattle cars on railroad trains, and taken to death camps in the East.

At Belsen, Germany, these women cook what they can find. They use the boots of the dead to fuel their cooking fire.

FRANCE: Of the 350,000 Jews living in France when Germany took over, half had recently moved there from Germany and Austria. Most of the French Jews lived in Paris. The rest were scattered throughout the country. As there were only 3,000 German police in France, they needed French help to round up the Jews. They had no trouble finding it. In six months in 1942, French police rounded up 42,500 Jews for deportation to the Auschwitz death camp. By the war's end 77,000 French Jews had been killed.

The Auschwitz death camp.

BELGIUM: About 66,000 Jews lived in Belgium when the Nazis invaded. Like France, most had recently moved there to escape the Nazis. In two years, from 1942 to 1944, 26,500 Jews were deported from Belgium and sent to Auschwitz.

THE NETHERLANDS: The Netherlands had long been a tolerant home to people of all religions and beliefs. There were 140,000 Jews living there when the Nazis swept into the country on May 10, 1940. In October 1942, deportation was begun. Over 110,000 Jews from the Netherlands were eventually killed. Many non-Jews in the Netherlands helped hide Jews from Nazi murder. One of the most famous Jewish children hidden was Anne Frank, who kept a diary of her experiences. She wrote:

> Our many Jewish friends are being taken away by the dozen. These people are treated by the Gestapo without a shred of decency, being loaded into cattle trucks. It is impossible to escape; most of the people in the camp are branded as inmates by their shaven heads. If it is as bad as this in Holland ('The Netherlands), whatever will it be like in the distant and barbarous regions they are sent to? We assume that most of them are murdered. The English radio speaks of their being gassed.

When Anne Frank was arrested by the Nazis on August 4, 1944, her diary was thrown on the floor by the SS. It was saved by a neighbor and published after the war. Today, *The Diary of Anne Frank* has sold more than twenty million copies in dozens of languages.

Like millions of other Jewish children, Anne Frank died by the hands of the Nazis. She and her family were sent to Auschwitz on September 3. Anne and her sister died of typhus on a forced death march only three weeks before the camp was liberated in 1945.

CHAPTER EIGHT

THE GHETTOS

*M*illions of Jews lived in Eastern Europe. Most of them lived in cities and towns where they made up a large portion of the population. Some towns in Lithuania and Poland were one-quarter to one-third Jews. When the Nazis invaded Poland, they forced all the Jews into ghettos surrounded by fences and guards. By 1942, all of the 3.5 million Jews in Poland were either jailed in ghettos, hiding out, or on the run.

The ghetto in Warsaw was surrounded by eleven miles of walls. So was the ghetto in Krakow. The ghetto in Lódz´ was enclosed by wooden fences and barbed wire. Some towns had open ghettos where people could come and go.

To the Nazis, ghettos were viewed as "Jewish residential quarters." But they were really holding pens for a population with no rights. They were a Nazi source of slave labor and wealth that could be stolen. Jews were uprooted from their homes and forced to move with whatever they could carry. Everything else they owned was taken by the Nazis.

Setting up ghettos was not easy. In the Lódz´ ghetto, 162,000 people were forced to live in an area where only 62,000 had lived before. Bus lines had to be rerouted. The main lines of trains that ran through the heart of the ghetto had to be walled off. In Warsaw 30 percent of the city's population were forced to live on 2 percent of its land.

Ghetto life was one of hunger, squalor, disease, and despair. Ten or fifteen people might live in an apartment meant for four. Food was denied to people who were forced to live on 1,100 calories a day. Diseases such as typhoid threatened everyone. Dead bodies were left on the street.

Still, the Jews tried to live their lives in peace. Schools were secretly set up to educate the children. Religious services were held. Theater, music, art, and poetry continued under the dark Nazi cloud of uncertainty and fear.

The ghettos were only a temporary solution to Hitler's "Jewish problem." Hans Biebow, the Nazi official who ran the Lódz´ ghetto said:

> I shall determine at which time and with what means the ghetto, and thereby the city of Lódz´ will be cleansed of Jews. In the end...we must burn out this bubonic plague.

By 1942 the Nazis had begun liquidating the ghettos of Eastern Europe. By 1944 more than two million Jews had been transferred to concentration camps. There were no more ghettos left.

CHAPTER NINE

THE WARSAW GHETTO

When Hitler invaded Poland, there were 375,000 Jews in Warsaw. Only New York City was home to more Jews. On November 16, 1940, the Warsaw ghetto was sealed by the Nazis. Their aim—mass starvation.

During 1941 one in ten people in the Warsaw ghetto died from starvation.

Still, people tried to survive. A vast network was set up by smugglers. Houses that butted up against the ghetto walls served as transfer points. Guards were bribed. Children learned to smuggle food. Even carts taking dead bodies to the cemetery came back with hidden food.

An underground press printed newspapers and bulletins. Historians recorded ghetto life for future generations. Orphanages were set up to care of the children whose parents had died.

During the summer of 1942, Nazis gave orders to round up more than 300,000 people in the ghetto. Soldiers went block to block, street to street, and finally house to house. Jews were loaded into cattle cars and taken by train to the death camp in Treblinka, sixty miles away.

CHAPTER TEN

THE MOBILE KILLING SQUADS

*O*n June 22, 1941, the German army swept into the Soviet Union. The Germans invaded in a two-thousand-mile-long front made up of three million soldiers. Soviet troops were overwhelmed. By September German troops were within 37 miles of Moscow. The entire government of the Soviet Union was dismantled, put on trains, and taken east to escape the Nazis. But when winter came, the Nazis got bogged down in frigid weather and snow. This was Hitler's first defeat.

The Nazi invasion of the Soviet Union was a turning point in the Holocaust. Wherever the Nazis went, mass killing was the policy of operations. Groups of SS soldiers followed the regular army and killed Jews wherever they were found.

Jews were easy to find. Nine out of ten lived in large cities. These were the first places the Nazi armies would invade

The mobile killing squads acted swiftly and without mercy. As soon as an area was invaded, the SS went into action. Jewish men, women, and children were rounded up. So were Soviet government officials, intellectuals, and Gypsies. The prisoners were marched to the edge of the city or town. Then they were stripped naked and shot. Their bodies were thrown into hastily dug mass graves.

The special death squads of the SS were called *Einsatzgruppen* or "special duty groups." These men were not German criminals, hoodlums, or psychopaths. They were ordinary citizens. Most were university-educated professional men.

A handful of men in the mobile killing squads asked to be relieved of their duties. The requests were granted and no action was taken against them. Most, however, simply did their job as they were ordered. Many drank heavily. They did not speak in terms of murder or killing. They used words like "cleansing," "executive measures," and "resettlement."

In some places, especially Lithuania and Latvia, local men were only too happy to help the Nazis with their grisly task. Jews were marched out of cities in long columns. They were instructed to bring their money, documents, valuables, and warm clothing.

A truck driver in Kiev describes the scene at a place called Babi Yar:

> I watched what happened when the Jews—men, women, and children—arrived. The [SS] led them past a number of different places where one after another they had to remove their luggage, then their coats, shoes, and overgarments and also underwear. They also had to leave their valuables in a designated place. There was a special pile for each article of clothing. I don't think it was even a minute from the time each Jew took off his coat before he was standing there completely naked.

> Once undressed, the Jews were led into the ravine which was about 150 meters long and 30 meters wide and a good 15 meters deep. When they reached the bottom of the ravine they were seized by members of the (police) and made to lie down on top of the Jews who had already been shot. A police marksman came along and shot each Jew in the neck with a submachine gun.

In the scene this truck driver witnessed, 33,771 Jews were killed in two days. This was done during the Jewish High Holy Days.

Some of the Einsatzgruppen complained about having to shoot women and children. They were provided with gas vans. These were regular trucks with the exhaust pipes re-directed into the cargo area. Jews were herded into these trucks ninety at a time. The trucks would then drive around until the diesel smoke had killed all the people in the back.

In other places Jews were marched into marshes and lakes to drown. In one killing in Romania, 20,000 Jews were rounded up, doused with gasoline, and set on fire.

Before the roving death squads were done, 1.2 million Jews had been killed, one by one. Their bodies were piled high in mass graves throughout the Nazi-occupied Soviet Union from Ukraine to the Baltic.

When the war turned against the Nazis, they went back to the murder sights and unearthed the graves. They burned the bodies to get rid of the evidence of their crimes. Sometimes this task took months.

These are the bodies of former prisoners of the Nazis in Nordhausen, Germany. These common graves were found all over Germany after the war.

CHAPTER ELEVEN

THE FINAL SOLUTION

*U*ntil 1939 the basic Nazi policy called for the forced-emigration of the Jews. That is, Hitler simply wanted them to move elsewhere—anywhere where the Germans didn't want to live. But by 1942, the Nazis had conquered most of Europe. The Jews had practically no where to go where the Nazis did not rule.

The mass-killing of Jews had begun in June 1941 when the Nazis took over portions of the Soviet Union. But these operations were done by mobile killing units. By December 1941 gas chambers were under construction at Auschwitz and Belzec concentration camps.

On January 20, 1942, top Nazi officials met in Wannsee, Germany, to plan the "Final Solution to the Jewish Problem." The Wannsee Conference was a turning point in an already grisly plan of extermination.

SS security officer Reinhard Heydrich called the conference. He invited the most brilliant and important fifteen officers of the government to a luxurious villa outside of Berlin. More than half the men invited held doctorates at Germany's finest universities. None of the men voiced any opposition to the planned mass murder. Butlers served fine brandy.

The decision was made to kill all the Jews and the policy was announced to the German government officials. Heydrich noted that the Final Solution would have to deal with eleven million Jews, including those in Britain and Ireland.

CHAPTER TWELVE

THE BUSINESS OF EXTERMINATION

*A*lthough there have been many instances of mass murder in history, the Holocaust was different. The Holocaust served no political purpose—the Jews were powerless against the Nazis and could do nothing to remove them from power. The Holocaust served no purpose of adding land to German territory—the Jews owned very little land and the Nazis had already taken over the countries of Europe. The murder of the Jews was nothing less than the total alteration of the human race.

The railroad tracks leading into Auschwitz death camp brought Jews to a horrible end. The Nazis performed their duty with swift purpose.

The destruction of the Jews became the national priority for the Nazis. This was in the face of any policy that made sense. Jews were murdered even though there was acute labor shortages. German manpower was used to hunt down every single Jew between Spain and Central Russia. Railroad trains were used to transport the Jews to death camps. This was done even though the German army desperately needed supplies to fight a war with the Soviet Union. The German legal system was tied up with laws, decrees, and official directives used to justify mass slaughter.

Nazi Germany became a state dedicated to the annihilation of the Jews. Every arm of the government needed to play a part. Parish churches provided the birth records of the Jews. The post offices mailed the notices of deportation. The Finance Ministry took Jewish wealth and property. Universities researched better and more efficient means to aid the slaughter.

These women are prisoners of Belson camp. Most are suffering from typhus, typhoid and dysentary. Hundreds died daily.

Government transportation bureaus paid for the trains that carried the Jews to their deaths. On every level of society, from highly paid officials, to drivers and postal carriers, the Germans took part in the Holocaust.

The Germans used their celebrated genius in business and technology to carry out Hitler's wishes. The locations of death camps were based on efficiency and low cost. German corporations made fortunes from the death industry. Drug firms tested drugs on inmates without regard to side effects. Companies bid on the contracts to build ovens and supply gas. Engineers designed ovens that could burn five hundred bodies an hour. The Final Solution was thought of by the Nazis as one of Germany's greatest achievements.

With mass murder, the Nazis reduced human bodies to natural resources with which to make money. Next to Auschwitz the industrial giant I. G. Farben ran a "factory" that removed raw materials from human bodies. Gold teeth were piled up to be melted down and sent to the treasury. Human hair was used to stuff mattresses. The ashes of the burned bodies became fertilizer. This "harvesting" of raw materials helped pay for the extermination. The Final Solution was run so that everyone made a monetary profit.

CHAPTER THIRTEEN

THE GHETTO UPRISING

*B*etween July and September 1942, over three hundred thousand Jews were shipped out of the Warsaw Ghetto. Their final destination was the death camp Treblinka. Only fifty-five thousand remained in the ghetto. The last to stay were determined to resist.

A group was formed called the Z.O.B. The letters stood for the Polish words meaning Jewish Fighting Organization. The Z.O.B. issued a proclamation:

> Jewish masses, the hour is drawing near. Not a single Jew should go to the railroad cars. Those who are unable to put up active resistance should resist passively, should go into hiding...Our slogan must be: All are ready to die as human beings.

On January 9, 1943, Himmler visited the Warsaw ghetto. He ordered another eight thousand Jews deported. Jews did not report as ordered. Many Jews went into hiding. There were armed battles in the streets. Many Jewish fighters were killed. Snipers shot at Nazi soldiers. The Nazis were sent running—for a time.

Many who remained thought that they had brought an end to the deportations. Hideouts were fortified. Jewish soldiers trained for the next battle without hope of rescue from the outside.

A major uprising began on April 19, the second night of the Jewish holiday of Passover. The Nazis invaded with a force of two thousand men, tanks, and flame-throwers.

The Jews fought back with a small arsenal of hand guns, machine guns, and bottles filled with flaming gasoline. Many were killed on both sides. The Nazis were finally turned back. The Jews celebrated.

More battles were fought with Nazi blood spilling in the street. At one point Nazi soldiers raised a white flag asking for a truce. The Jews responded with a volley of gun fire.

The Nazis cut off electricity, water, and gas to the ghetto. Police dogs were brought in to find people in hiding. When Jews hid in the sewers, the Nazis flooded them. The Nazis began to burn the ghetto, building by building. But for more than a month, Jews held out against the Nazis.

In the end, the Nazis did triumph. Many of the resistance fighters saved their last bullets to commit suicide. Seven thousand Jews were shot in the streets, seven thousand were sent to Treblinka, and fifteen thousand were sent to the death camp at Lublin. The ghetto was destroyed.

CHAPTER FOURTEEN

THE TRAINS OF DEATH

*R*ailroad trains were the main link in the extermination of the Jews. Trains from every corner of Nazi-occupied Europe brought human cargo to the death camps that were built along the rail lines. The German railroad, the *Reichsbahn*, employed 1.4 million workers who kept the death trains in operation. The worker's jobs were to obtain freight cars, plan schedules, keep the tracks open and maintained, drive the locomotives, and clean the cars.

As the war continued, there was a shortage of rail cars. Trains were needed to supply soldiers on the front. Allied bombing raids cut off service. But the trains carrying Jews continued to roll. As the shortage became worse, more Jews were crammed into fewer trains on slower routes. One hundred people were jammed like cattle into one freight car. Typical trains pulled two hundred such cars. The weight of these 20,000 people slowed the travel to thirty miles per hour.

The Holocaust was no secret to the rail workers. But no railroad workers resigned or protested. At Auschwitz alone, there were forty-four tracks in a row. That is twice the amount as New York's Pennsylvania Station.

The SS used travel agents to book one-way passage to the death camps. The agents were paid four pennies per kilometer of track that each Jew would travel. Children under ten rode for half price. Those under four rode for free. A group rate was offered for deportations of more than four hundred people. The Reichsbahn used the same forms and procedures to send Jews to Auschwitz as they did to book tourists going on vacation.

Jews were transported to the death camps on trains that ran as efficiently as possible.

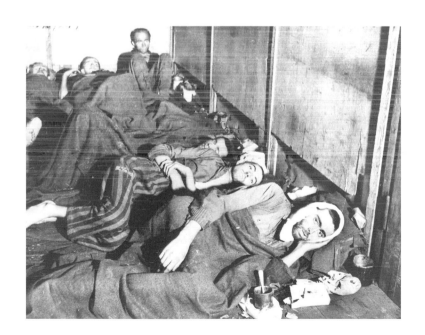

The prisoners were crammed together in dirty facilities without food or medical attention.

The scale of these deportations was enormous. Between May 15 and July 9, 1944, over 434,000 Hungarian Jews from fifty-five depots were deported to Auschwitz on 147 trains. The railway system was stretched to the limit to keep up with the demand of the camps where 12,000 people a day were gassed.

The Nazis did their best to hide their deeds from the victims. Jews were told that they were going to "resettlements in the East." They were told they were going to labor camps. Jews were asked to bring their belongings. It seemed to work. Even as late as 1944, many Jews had never heard of Auschwitz.

The journey was agonizing. The trip might take seven to ten days. In summer the cattle cars were unbearably hot. In the winter, they were freezing. There was no food and no water for drinking or bathing. There were no toilets and people were forced to stand in their bodily wastes. The stench was overwhelming. When the doors finally opened, the passengers who lived through the ordeal thought that the worst was over.

One survivor of the nightmare wrote:

> We suffered from thirst and cold: at every stop we clamored for water, or even a handful of snow, but we were rarely heard: the soldiers of the escort drove off anybody who tried to approach the convoy. Two young mothers, nursing their children, groaned night and day, begging for water...The hours of darkness were nightmares without end. Everyone said farewell to life....

> The climax came suddenly. The door opened with a crash, and the dark echoed with the outlandish orders in that curt, barbaric barking of Germans in command. A vast platform appeared before us, lit up by reflectors. A little beyond it, a row of lorries (trucks)...A dozen SS men...began to

interrogate us..."How old? Healthy or ill?" and on the basis of reply they pointed us in two different directions.

The different directions had the meaning of life or death. Ninety percent of the Jews were gassed immediately. The ones who were pointed in the other direction were to become the slave laborers.

CHAPTER FIFTEEN

LIFE IN THE DEATH CAMPS

*T*he busy Germans built over nine thousand concentration camps in Europe. The camps were first used as giant prisons. Some were used for special projects such as using slave labor to build bombs for the war efforts. Finally they were used for murder.

There were transit camps, prisoner-of-war camps, police detention camps, work-education camps, orphan camps, and private-industry camps. There were more than three hundred camps for women only.

Six camps served as the main killing centers, all in Poland: Treblinka, Sobibór, Belzec, Chelmno, Auschwitz/Birkenau, and Majdanek. The last two were also slave labor camps. In 1942 the camps held 100,000 inmates. In 1943 they held 224,000. In 1944 they held 524,000 inmates. By January 1945 they held 714,000 inmates, of which 200,000 were women. More than three million Jews were murdered in these camps. Some died from starvation, exhaustion, and disease. Many more were killed by gas.

A grim reminder of the Nazis' extermination camp. This is a canister of poisonous Zyklon B gas used at Auschwitz to kill millions of Jews.

German scientists searched for the cheapest means of killing the most people. After experimenting with a variety of gases, they settled on an insecticide called Zyklon B (Cyclone B).

The killing was carried out with startling efficiency.

More than 870,000 Jews were killed at Treblinka with a staff of 150 people. Most of the workers were Ukrainian. There were fewer than one hundred known survivors of Treblinka.

In eight months 600,000 Jews and 3,000 Gypsies were murdered in Belzec. Only a handful survived.

At Majdanek over 500,000 people from twenty-eight countries and fifty-four ethnic groups were killed. More than 60 percent were non-Jewish Poles.

At Birkenau (Auschwitz II) over 1.1 million Jews were murdered in addition to 20,000 Poles, 19,000 Gypsies, and 12,000 Russian prisoners of war.

CHAPTER SIXTEEN

THE SELECTION

*A*t the entrance to each death camp, the doors were opened on the cattle cars. The dead fell out like cord wood. Those living and able to walk were sent on. Those who could not walk were taken to the gas chambers immediately. The walkers then came to the first *Selektion* or Selection. Pregnant women, small children, the sick, and the old were immediately condemned to death. Men were separated from women and their valuables were taken. They were forced to undress and marched to the gas chambers. The Nazis kept up the charade until the end. The gas chambers were labeled "showers."

Those selected to work were registered. Then their heads were shaved and numbers were tattooed on their arms. They were given black-and-white striped uniforms. Soon the living would envy those who were killed immediately.

The laborers lived in constant fear of other "selections." Every day, they were forced to run naked in front of SS officers to show that they still had strength. The officers stood with a stick and directed the runners into this line or that. One line went to the gas chambers. The runners did not know which one. The living would return to the barracks to live another day.

CHAPTER SEVENTEEN

THE SLAVES

*B*y 1942, the Nazis had over seven million slaves working for them. The slave laborers worked eleven-hour shifts with almost no food. In the winter they were not given warm clothing. The most respected German corporations used slave labor, including BMW, Siemens, Daimler-Benz (Mercedes-Benz), Messerschmitt, and Krupp. The executives who ran these corporations were not forced to use slaves. They just did it as a "good business practice." I. G. Farben invested more than 700 million *Reichsmarks* (German dollars) to build a huge petrochemical plant at Auschwitz III, staffed by human slaves.

CHAPTER EIGHTEEN

LIFE AND DEATH AT AUSCHWITZ

*A*uschwitz was the largest and most highly organized death camp in history. It was actually three camps: a concentration camp, a death camp, and a slave labor camp. It was in a zone of nineteen square miles and was guarded by 6,000 men. The guards were in the Nazi SS Death's Head Units. They had been in charge of concentration camps since 1934 and wore skull and bones insignias on their black shirts.

The death camps were inhumane. Hundreds of people were crammed into small areas without heat, plumbing or electricity.

The concentration camp was located in the Polish town of Oswiecim. It was opened in June 1940 with 728 Polish prisoners on the sight of an Austrian military barracks. By 1945 more than 1.25 million people had been killed there and 100,000 worked as slave laborers.

A sign above Auschwitz read "Work Liberates." One survivor of Auschwitz was fifteen-years-old when she arrived. Later she wrote:

> How does one describe walking into Auschwitz, the smell? And someone pointing out to you that those are gas chambers, that your parents went up in smoke. When I asked, "When will I see my mother?" several hours after I came into the camp, I was shown the smoke. That is how I found out where she went.

The camp was laid out in two- or three-story brick buildings in endless rows. The streets were cobblestone. Electrical fences and a network of canals thirteen miles long surrounded the camps. Chains of guard posts two-thirds of a mile out from the fences added another layer of security. The area between was patrolled by SS and police dogs.

One block was the sight of bizarre medical experiments. Thousands of prisoners were sterilized using radiation. Dr. Josef Mengele performed horrible medical experiments on children. The Nazis studied twins, the disabled, and others in breeding experiments. Prisoners were frozen or injected with poisons to see what would happen to them.

Every day at roll call those who were sick or could not stand up were killed. Six people slept on a plank of wood. If one turned over, everyone would have to turn over. There were no covers, no pillows, and no mattresses. One barn, originally built to hold forty-eight horses, housed eight hundred people. Five hundred people lived in one block with neither a lavatory nor a washbowl between them. Only one bucket was available for a toilet. Until 1943 there was one water tap. Sickness and diseases were rampant.

The Auschwitz death camp, where millions of Jews perished.

CHAPTER NINETEEN

THE SHOWERS

*T*he Nazis killed their victims with a common pesticide, prussic acid, known as Zyklon B. Of course no one would walk willingly to their deaths so the Nazis labeled the gas chambers as "showers." On the entrance to the chambers signs read: "To the baths and disinfecting rooms." Notices read: "Cleanliness brings freedom!"

Men, women, and children were led into rooms to undress. They were told to tie their shoes together and fold their clothes neatly into a pile. Once the victims were nude, they were herded into the gas chambers. Women and children were the majority, and they went first. Fake showerheads in the ceiling kept up the deception. The room was sealed and locked. The gas was discharged into the vents and the screaming and gasping for air began. Within twenty minutes, everyone lay dead.

After the gas, men were sent in to load the bodies on elevators. Gold teeth were extracted and women's hair was shaved from the dead bodies. Ten or fifteen bodies were transported at a time in elevators to the ovens above. The chambers at Auschwitz/Birkenau could kill six thousand people a day.

When Soviet troops entered Birkenau on January 18, 1945, they found 358,000 men's suits, 837,000 women's outfits, and 15,400 pounds of human hair packed into paper bags. All was saved in warehouses for further use by the Nazis.

CHAPTER TWENTY

BEAUTIFUL HAIR

*U*pon arrival at a death camp, most victims were immediately sent to the gas chambers. Those who weren't were dehumanized and humiliated. They were tattooed with numbers. One survivor tells of his arrival at Auschwitz as a teenager.:

> As you stretched out your arm, they gave you a number.... And as they gave me my tattoo number, B-4990, the SS man came to me, and he says to me, "Do you know what this number's all about?" I said, "No, sir." "Okay, let me tell you now. You are being dehumanized."

Then began the taking of the hair. One worker describes the scene:

> A big transport came in from Hungary. Beautiful people with beautiful long hair.... The music started playing, women were singing [at the entrance to Auschwitz, a small orchestra of pretty young women played music to lull the suspicions of the new arrivals]. And we knew right away what was going to happen to them. Beautiful people. All dressed up so nice with jewelry and everything.

> It didn't take long. They took their clothes, they cut their hair, they put everything in a pile... Some of them had such beautiful long hair. They must have taken maybe two or three hundreds of them. They cut their hair and took everything away...

Camp commanders were informed that "human hair will be processed into felt to be used in industry, and thread will be spun out of them. The combed-out and cut-off women's hair will be used to make socks for the submarine crews, and to manufacture felt stockings for the railroad workers."

Hair was also used for ignition mechanisms in bombs, ropes and cords for ships, and for stuffing mattresses. Camp commanders were required to submit monthly reports on the amount of hair collected.

CHAPTER TWENTY ONE

DEATH MARCHES

*I*n the winter of 1944, the Nazis knew that they had lost the war. The Soviet army was closing in from the east. The British and Americans were closing in from the west. The SS were desperately trying to get rid of the concentration camps. They wanted no eyewitnesses to their crimes against humanity. They began to put as much effort into destroying the camps that they had into building them. Still, the Nazis pressed on to complete the Final Solution.

The inmates of camps were moved westward in the dead of winter. The Nazis figured if the prisoners were in the heartland of Germany, it would look better, as if the killing was limited to Germany.

In January 1945, with the Soviet army only six hours away, sixty-six thousand prisoners were marched out of Auschwitz.

The prisoners were loaded on trains to the camps in Gross-Rosen, Buchenwald, Dachau, and Mauthausen. Seventeen thousand died on this trip.

On January 20, seven thousand Jews, six thousand of them women, were marched out of satellite camps in the Danzig region. They marched for ten days in snow and slush, from first light until darkness. Each night the marchers were ordered to take a left turn, walk twenty paces and lay down. At dawn, those who could not rise were shot. Along the way, seven hundred were murdered when they fell by the wayside. Those who lived were marched off a cliff into the Baltic Sea and shot. There were only thirteen survivors.

One survivor of the camps, Primo Levi, wrote about his shoes:

> Death begins with the shoes; for the most of us, they show themselves to be instruments of torture, which after a few hours of marching cause painful sores which finally become infected. Whoever has them is forced to walk as if dragging a convict's chain...his feet swell and the more they swell the more friction with the wood and the cloth of the shoes....

Another victim wrote:

> Like nearly all camp inmates...my legs were so swollen and the skin on them so tightly stretched that I could scarcely bend my knees. I had to leave my shoes unlaced in order to make them fit my swollen feet. There would not have been space for socks even if I had any.... So my bare feet were always wet and my shoes always full of snow.... Every single step became real torture.

In 1944, impatient Nazis could not wait for trains to arrive in

Budapest, Hungary, to take the Jews away. On November 8, a death march began with tens of thousands of Hungarian men, women, and children. They were marched to Austria. Many died from starvation, cold, and exhaustion. The march lasted a month. Those who lived were killed at Dachau and Mauthausen.

In all, there were fifty-nine different death marches from concentration camps during that final winter of Nazi occupation. Some marches were hundreds of miles long. The prisoners were given little or no food or water. Those who could not march were shot on the spot.

CHAPTER TWENTY TWO

THE END OF THE NIGHTMARE

On January 27, 1945, the Soviet army entered Auschwitz. They found that the Germans had neglected to burn piles of human hair, tin cups, eyeglasses, pots and pans, baby carriages and other possessions. They found 836,255 women's dresses, 348,000 men's suits, and 38,000 pairs of men's shoes.

In Germany, Allied troops were winning ground and liberating camps. Between April 11 and 28, American and British soldiers liberated Buchenwald, Dachau, Bergen-Belsen and other death camps. The same sights greeted the liberators—piles of corpses and dazed skeletons walking about. The scene was so grisly that U. S. General George Patton would not enter the camps for fear of becoming sick to his stomach.

British troops liberating Bergen-Belsen found that the Nazis had experimented there using human skin for lampshades.

Dauchau concentration camp survivors line the fence to cheer the American forces that liberated them.

This photo is a gruesome reminder of the death camps—a vast pile of shoes worn by the men, women, and children who marched through the portals of the annihilation camps and into oblivion. Every size of footwear is represented here, ranging from heavy military boots to tiny infant sandals.

CHAPTER TWENTY THREE

THE END OF HITLER

*A*s the Allied army advanced on Berlin, Hitler retreated to a bomb-shelter fifty feet below the ground. On April 22, 1945, the Soviets were in Berlin. Hitler was near hysteria. His lieutenants were fleeing the country.

In his final hours, Hitler married his long-time companion Eva Braun. After the ceremony Hitler dictated his final testament:

> I charge the (new) leaders of (Germany) and those under them to...observe the laws of race and to mercilessly oppose the universal poisoner of all peoples, international Jewry.

So, with his country in flaming ruins, and 40 million people killed in a war he started, Hitler's last words still dripped hatred for the Jews.

Shortly afterward Hitler shot himself in the mouth. Eva Braun took cyanide. Their bodies were burned. Hitler and his twisted dreams of the Final Solution were dead.

On May 7, 1945 the Nazis surrendered to the Allies. The nightmare of World War II was over in Europe.

CHAPTER TWENTY FOUR

THE DEATH COUNT

*S*ix million is the minimum number of Jews killed by the Nazis. Thousands of infants and babies were killed before their births could be recorded. Today throughout Europe monuments and gravestones can be found for the victims. The stones mark mass graves of people about whom nothing will ever be known: not their names, not their ages, not their birthplaces, or even their total number. The following are the estimates of those killed, country by country and region by region:

Atrocities at Belsen death camp, Belsen, Germany. Bodies piled one upon the other is the scene many Allied soldiers saw when they liberated the camps.

Albania: 200

Austria: 65,000

Belgium: 40,387

Bessarabia: 200,000

Bukovina: 124,632

Bulgaria: 14,000

Crete: 260

Czechoslovakia: 217,000

Danzig: 1,000

Denmark: 77

Estonia: 1,000

Finland: 11

France: 90,000

Germany: 160,000

Greece: 65,000

Holland: 106,000

Hungary: 450,000

Italy: 8,000

Kos: 120

Latvia: 80,000

Libya: 562

Lithuania: 135,000

Luxembourg: 700

Macedonia: 7,122

Memel: 8,000

Norway: 728

Poland: 3,000,000

Rhodes: 1,700

Rumania: 300,000

Ruthenia: 60,000

Soviet Union: 1,240,000

Thrace: 4,221

Transylvania: 105,000

Yugoslavia: 26,000

CHAPTER TWENTY FIVE

THE SURVIVORS

*T*here were over 300,000 survivors of the concentration camps. Over 1.5 million Jews survived Hitler's efforts to destroy them. Some escaped from Europe. Some Polish Jews hid in Soviet Central Asia. More than 20,000 French, Dutch, and Belgian Jews found refuge in Spain, Portugal, and Switzerland. Denmark's Jews had been smuggled to safety in Sweden. Some Jews were saved because they were sheltered by non-Jews who risked their lives to help them. This is a partial list of the survivors:

Albania: 200	Germany: 30,000
Austria: 7,000	Greece: 12,000
Baltic States (Lithuania, Latvia, and Estonia): 25,000	Holland: 20,000
Belgium: 25,000	Hungary: 20,000
	Italy: 32,000
Bulgaria: 50,000	Luxembourg: 4,000
Crete: 7	Norway: 1,000
Czechoslovakia: 44,000	Poland: 225,000
Danzig: 8,000	Rhodes: 161
Denmark: 5,500	Rumania: 300,000
Finland: 2,000	Soviet Union: 300,000
France: 200,000	Yugoslavia: 12,000

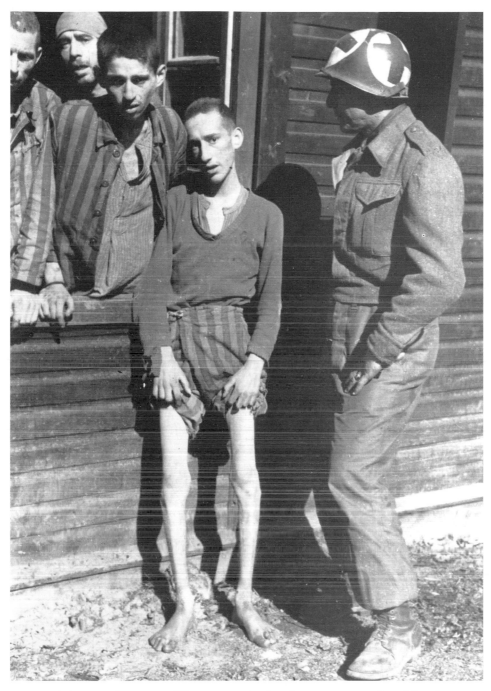

These prisoners of Langenstein death camp were freed by the U.S. Ninth Army Forces. The prisoners suffered horrible abuses and managed to survive.

CHAPTER TWENTY SIX

RETURNING TO LIFE

*N*ow that the Jews had been liberated from the camps, a new struggle was beginning. These people had lost their families and their homes. They had no place to go, nobody was waiting for them anywhere. Still, there was joy at even the simplest things—water, tables, chairs, a clean bed with sheets and pillows, food.

Some died from overeating the sweets and chocolates provided by the friendly soldiers.

Some described the liberation as a dream. No longer were orders shouted at them. There was no more work, no more blows, no more roll calls.

None of the survivors ever forgot his or her time spent in the Nazi nightmare. Some felt guilty that they had lived when so many had died.

CHAPTER TWENTY SEVEN

IN THE END

*A*dolf Hitler, the Nazis, and the German people killed two-thirds of the Jews living in Europe. They were helped by killers in each nation that they occupied. In Poland, Lithuania, Latvia, and Czechoslovakia 90 percent of the Jews were exterminated. Worlds were shattered. The center of Jewish life had now shifted to the United States and Israel. The ashes of the dead were all that remained of two thousand years of Jewish culture.

The human language had no words to describe the Nazi horror. Words like holocaust, genocide, atrocity, extermination, annihilation came in to use to describe the events. The Jews call the event Shoah. The word appears three times in the Bible, referring each time to a place that had been brought to waste and ruin.

Although the numbers are mind-boggling, each number was an individual human being—the same as any of us. Behind each number was a pair of eyes, a face, love, and sorrow.

The killers were men and women from a highly civilized country. Their deeds were human evil that was magnified by the power of the state. It was an evil fueled by science and technology. There were no moral, social, religious, or political controls to stop it.

The United States, the Soviet Union, Great Britain, and France brought leading Nazis to trail. They charged them with crimes against humanity. The trials were held in Nuremberg, where Hitler had passed the original laws to target the Jews.

Hundreds of witnesses testified. Blueprints of the gas chambers were found. Secret German documents were produced. One general bragged at the trial, "We executed 400,000 Hungarian Jews alone." He was hanged at Auschwitz. Many other Nazis were also hanged. Some are still being tried today.

On May 14, 1948, the Jews proclaimed their own country—Israel. Although the Arabs who lived there opposed the idea, today Israel exists as a home for all the Jews of the world.

Hitler believed that Nazi Germany would live for one thousand years. It lasted only twelve. Before the war there were forty-five hundred Jewish communities in twenty countries. All were active centers of Jewish learning and thought. Hitler erased those communities from the map of the world. Six million Jews disappeared.

About the Holocaust, historian Yehuda Bauer stated three commandments that humans must carry out:

"Thou shalt not be a victim."

"Thou shalt not be a perpetrator."

"Above all, thou shalt not be a bystander."

In the words of one who was there:

I have told you this story not to weaken you

But to strengthen you.

Now it is up to you.

Dachau concentration camp inmates cheer upon liberation by the U.S. 7th Army, April 1945.

GLOSSARY

Abominable - very bad or hateful.

Allies - the United States, the Soviet Union, Great Britain, France, Canada, and the other countries who came together to fight Germany, Italy, and Japan in World War II.

Annihilate - to reduce to complete ruin, to wipe out completely.

Anti-Semitism - hatred of Jews.

Appeasement - to pacify in an effort to bring peace.

Aryan - people of Northern European descent.

Atrocity - a shockingly bad or atrocious act.

Concentration camp - a guarded camp for the detention and forced labor of political prisoners.

Conspiracy - an evil, unlawful plot.

Cremate, crematoria - to cremate is to burn a dead body; this is done in a crematorium; more than one crematorium are crematoria.

Dehumanize - to take away human qualities.

Deportation - to expel from a city, region, or country.

Descendant - one descended from another or from a common stock.

Einsatzgruppen - special duty groups. The name given to the Nazi mobile killing squads in Eastern Europe.

Emigrate - to leave one country and settle in another.

Exterminate - to destroy totally.

Genetics - the science of heredity.

Gestapo - the German state secret police.

Ghetto - a section of a city in most European countries where all Jews were forced to live.

Holocaust - the mass extermination of Jews in Nazi Germany.

Liberate - to free.

Liquidating - getting rid of, especially by killing.

Myth - a legend or story, usually one that attempts to account for something in nature.

Passover - A Jewish holiday celebrating the deliverance of the Hebrews from slavery in ancient Egypt.

Persecution - to be harassed with harsh treatment because of one's race, religion, or beliefs.

Pious - religious.

Prejudice - hatred or dislike of someone because of their race, religion, or beliefs.

Propaganda - information or ideas that are repeated over and over to change the public's thinking about an idea or group of people.

Protocol - an original draft of a document.

Racist - a person who believes that their race is superior to others.

Reichstag - the ruling body, congress, or parliament of Germany.

Repress - to keep under control or stifle another person.

Schutzstaffel (SS) - the black-shirted security squad of elite Nazis.

Segregate - to separate a group of people because of their race, religion, or beliefs.

Semite - a member of any of a various ancient and modern people, especially Hebrews or Arabs.

Swastika - an ancient figure made of a cross with its arms bent at right angles. Native Americans take this symbol to mean good luck. The Nazis used it for their national symbol.

Synagogue - a Jewish house of worship.

Zyklon B - prussic acid, the insecticide used to gas people in the death camps.

BIBLIOGRAPHY

Adler, David A. *We Remember the Holocaust.* New York: Henry Holt and Company, 1989.

Aharoni, Yohanan, and Avi-Yonah, Michael. *The Macmillan Bible Atlas.* New York: Macmillan, 1993.

Ausubel, Nathan, and Gross, David C. *Pictorial History of the Jewish People.* New York: Crown Publishers, Inc., 1953, 1984.

Berenbaum, Michael. *The World Must Know.* Boston: Little, Brown and Company, 1993.

Block, Gay, and Drucker. *Malka Rescuers.* New York: Holmes & Meier Publications, Inc., 1992

Chaikin, Miriam. *A Nightmare in History: The Holocaust 1933-1945.* New York: Clarion Books, 1987.

Dawidowicz, Lucy S. *The War Against the Jews 1933-1945.* New York: Seth Press, 1986.

de Lange, Nicholas. *Atlas of the Jewish World.* New York: Facts on File Publications, 1984.

Flannery, Edward H. *The Anguish of the Jews.* New York: Paulist Press, 1985.

Friedman, Ina R. *The Other Victims.* Boston: Houghton Mifflin Company, 1990.

Gilbert, Martin. *Final Journey.* New York: Mayflower Books, 1979.

Gilbert, Martin. *The Macmillan Atlas of the Holocaust.* New York: Macmillan, 1982.

Greenfeld, Howard. *The Hidden Children.* New York: Ticknor & Fields, 1993.

Landau, Elaine. *The Warsaw Ghetto Uprising.* New York: New Discovery Books, 1992.

Paldiel, Mordecai. *The Path of the Righteous.* Hoboken, New Jersey: KTAV Publishing House, Inc., 1993.

Index